Money Maker

A Step-by-Step Guide on Investing for Beginners

David Weekly

David Weekly

Copyright 2016 - All rights reserved.

This document is geared towards providing exact and reliable information in regards to the topic and issue covered. The publication is sold with the idea that the publisher is not required to render accounting, officially permitted, or otherwise, qualified services. If advice is necessary, legal or professional, a practiced individual in the profession should be ordered.

From a Declaration of Principles which was accepted and approved equally by a Committee of the American Bar Association and a Committee of Publishers and Associations.

In no way is it legal to reproduce, duplicate, or transmit any part of this document in either electronic means or in printed format. Recording of this publication is strictly prohibited and any storage of this document is not allowed unless with written permission from the publisher. All rights reserved.

The information provided herein is stated to be truthful and consistent, in that any liability, in terms of inattention or otherwise, by any usage or abuse of any policies, processes, or directions contained within is the solitary and utter responsibility of the recipient reader. Under no circumstances will any legal responsibility or blame be held against the publisher for any reparation, damages, or monetary loss due to the information herein, either directly or indirectly.

Respective authors own all copyrights not held by the publisher.

Money Maker

The information herein is offered for informational purposes solely, and is universal as so. The presentation of the information is without contract or any type of guarantee assurance.

The trademarks that are used are without any consent, and the publication of the trademark is without permission or backing by the trademark owner. All trademarks and brands within this book are for clarifying purposes only and are the owned by the owners themselves, not affiliated with this document.

David Weekly

Content

Introduction	v
Step 1: Get Your Personal Finances In Order	1
Step 2: Learn The Basics Of Investing	11
Step 3: Set Investment Goals	19
Step 4: Determine Your Risk Tolerance	33
Step 5: Find Your Investment Style	39
Step 6: Know The Associated Costs In Investment	48
Step 7: Find Your Investment Advisor	53
Step 8: Choose Your Investments	58
Step 9: Review Your Investments	68
Conclusion	73

Introduction

I want to thank you and congratulate you for purchasing this book…

"Money Maker: A Step-by-Step Guide on Investing for Beginners"

Investing is really easy as long as you know the steps of how you can put your money to work for you. There is no need to work overtime hours or to take another job just to increase your income. There are various ways to grow your money through investments like buying equities, trading bonds, investing in mutual funds or buying real estate. But these investments carry risks, because you could lose all your money if you are not careful in choosing your investments. That's why I have written this book to guide you in the process of investing as well as provide you important pointers to avoid losing your capital.

In this book you can learn how you can invest even if you have debt, how to set your investment goals, how to determine your risk tolerance, how to find your investment style, how to shop around for your financial advisor, which investments to choose, and many more!

David Weekly

Money Maker

David Weekly

David Weekly

Step 1: Get Your Personal Finances In Order

Getting into investing without first assessing your finances is like exploring a jungle without any basic survival skills. Aside from your daily expenses, payments to loans and credit card balances could easily eat up the amount of money left for investment.

Before you jump right in, you first need to learn how you can invest on a tight budget, and decide whether it is ideal according to your circumstances to start investing or pay off debt first.

Investing on a Tight Budget

Fortunately, you don't need a large amount to start investing. Probably, you already heard about the mantra of "paying yourself first", but this is easier said than done. The high cost of living, as well as the unplanned expenses, which may seem to spring up from nowhere could make any individual feel that saving for investment is difficult - if not impossible.

Below are ideal ways you can follow to set aside extra money without breaking your pockets so you can begin investing.

David Weekly

Saving Is Possible and Easy

Investing is easy if you have enough excess cash. But not everyone has extra money available for investment. Investing and saving require dedication, but it doesn't need to be laborious. There are new ways that can help you to save and invest. Many banks in the US are offering automatic debit arrangement, which will take a fixed amount of money regularly from your account, which is more effective than setting aside cash later for deposit.

Another easy way to save is to use any bonuses you have received every year as well as any tax rebates for investment instead of spending it on unnecessary items. This is a great way to increase your investment funds and earn rewards.

Invest In Your Company's 401(k)

It is ideal to participate in your company's 401(k) plan, specifically if your employer matches your contributions. However, you should be cautious in this option. It is always ideal to be a wise investor and understand the prospectus. if the company's 401(k) cannot go beyond the 500 S&P return rate, then it might be more beneficial to invest the money on your own.

Thousands of companies in the US have not regularly beaten the 500 S&P, which is an index of the 500 biggest companies in the US. Searching the different options may not take long. Nevertheless, it is crucial to maximize your returns. Be sure to re-evaluate your plan to make certain that your fund can meet your investment goals. Previous performance is a good indicator of what could happen in the future, but don't take it as a guarantee.

Many websites offer reliable resources to help you learn about the past performance of a certain company's stock. However, you should also assess the performance of the mutual funds. Take note that the performance of the fund is a crucial part of the equation. You should also look out for costly administrative fees.

David Weekly

What to Do If You Don't Have 401(k) Plan?

Millions of Americans are working for small companies that do not offer any form of savings plan. However, this doesn't mean that they cannot save and invest on their own. Here are alternatives that you can try:

Exchange Traded Funds

If the concept of choosing your own stocks is a bit fearsome to you and you don't have enough funds to get the services of an investment advisor, you should not worry, because there is a solution. You can buy certain Exchange Traded Funds (ETFs) that are similar to index mutual funds, but traded like stocks.

Investing in ETFs will not only give you the chance to obtain one investment that involves different stocks, it will also give you the opportunity to diversify your investments. There are numerous options for ETFs, just like mutual funds. Hence, it must be easier to look for an ETF, which signifies the market goals that you are searching for.

Looking for different ETFs and their performance can be easy thanks to the available financial websites. You can look for every ETF by entering their ticker symbol, and you can access data tidbits within seconds.

Web Brokers Offering Automatic Investing Options

If you think that you are ready to invest, you should look for affordable web brokerages. Many online companies are offering automatic investing plans, separate one-time trading on stocks and a money market account with affordable rates. Many companies are allowing no minimum on the investment you can open, so you could start investing any amount that you are comfortable with.

With hard work and the right information, it is easy to invest and earn sizeable profits. Many successful investors started with a few dollars. Hence, you should remember that it is not the amount of dollars that you can invest that matters. It is all about how you can start investing. In view of this, using some of the pointers that you will learn in this book can provide you an opportunity to convert pennies into shares that you can save for future expenses.

Beginning even with a minimum investment can give you the chance to grow your portfolio. After all, great trees grow from small seeds. As a beginner in the world of investing, you can have all the time and information by your side.

Which Should Come First? Reduce Debt or Investment

Young investors usually face the dilemma of whether to invest excess money of use it to pay down debt. But you should remember that if you put all of your money in paying debt, you may not accumulate enough assets that you can use for your retirement. On the other hand, if you are too aggressive in investments, you could lose everything you have.

To help you decide between investment or debt reduction, you should look into certain factors such as your cash flow, risk tolerance, and investment choices.

Cash Flow

Financial experts usually recommend that regular employees should have a minimum of six month worth of monthly expenses in liquid (cash) and a debt-to-income ratio of not higher than 33% debt to income ratio. Before you reduce debt or start investing, you should first establish a cushion, so that you can survive through any rough circumstances that you may face in your life.

After saving enough for unexpected expenses, the next step is to pay off any credit card debt that you have accumulated. This debt often carries an interest rate that is often higher than what most investments could earn prior to taxes. Hence, if your debt to income ratio is way too high, you should concentrate first on settling your payables before you start investing. Once you have set aside enough emergency fund and you have enough debt to income ration, you can invest with more confidence.

Bear in mind that some fort of debt like your mortgage is not for your disadvantage. If your credit score is high, your after-tax profits on investments can also be higher compared to your after-tax expenses of debt within your mortgage.

In addition, because of the tax benefits to retirement investing, and with the fact that most companies are matching their staff contributions to certain retirement plans, it makes a lot of sense to invest than paying down other forms of debt like vehicle loans.

If you are a small business owner or you are self-employed, having enough cash for your daily expenses and for emergencies could make or break your career. For instance, if a self-employed person with a very tight cash flow could easily acquire a windfall of $20,000, but he could also have $20,000 outstanding debt. One payable has a balance of $6,000 at a 5% rate, and the other is $12,000 at a 7% interest rate.

While the entrepreneur could pay off these payables, he has decided to settle only one payable to preserve the cash. The $6,000 note has $129 monthly payments, while the $12,000 has $98 monthly payments. Conventional financial advisors may suggest that he should pay off first the $12,000 note first because of the higher interest rate. But in this case, it may make sense to settle the one that is providing the higher cash flow. Hence, paying off the $6,000 instantly will add more than $130 per month to the cash flow of the business. The remaining

$12,000 could be used to expand the business or as a standby fund for emergency expenses.

Risk Tolerance

Consider the following when determining your risk tolerance:

- Income
- Age
- Time horizon
- Earning power
- Tax status

For instance, if you are still young and you still have the capacity to earn money that could be lost and you have a high excess income relative to your lifestyle, you can have a higher risk tolerance and you can afford to invest with more confidence compared to paying off debt. If you have more pressing issues like high cost of healthcare, you may also choose to set aside paying down debt at the moment.

Instead of investing the disposable income in high-risk assets like equities, you can also choose to keep higher allocations in fixed-income investments. The longer your time horizon is until you retire, the higher potential return you can enjoy when you invest instead of paying off your debt. This is because equities could return 10% or more in the long run.

Another important factor in assessing risk tolerance is your willingness to take risk. Where you are in this range could help you in deciding what you can do. If you are trying to be aggressive in your investments, you may like to invest your disposable income instead of paying down debt. If you are averse to risk, or you are not comfortable in losing money through investments and you don't like any type of debt, it is ideal for you to use your extra income to pay all your debts.

But you should remember that this strategy can have a setback. For example, while you may think that paying off debt is a conservative strategy, paying off but not getting rid of debt, could even turn into the opposite of what you have to achieve. For instance, an investor who wants to pay off his mortgage may leave him with very thin financial reserves may also regret the decision if he suddenly lost his regular source of income and still need to pay off high mortgage payments.

Investment Choices

From a numerical perspective, you should not base your decision on your after-tax expenses of borrowing than your after-tax return on investing. Let's say that you are earning a regular salary with a 30% tax bracket and you have a regular 30-year mortgage with 5% interest rate. Since it is allowed to deduce mortgage interest on your taxes, your actual after-tax cost of debt can be lower.

If you are holding a diversified investment portfolio, which involves both fixed income and equities, you may discover that your after-tax profit on the money you have invested could be higher than the after-tax payment for your debt.

For instance, if your mortgage is at a lower interest rate and you have invested in securities with higher risk like a small cap stocks value, investing will be the better choice.

If you are self-employed, you can also choose to invest in your business instead of deducting your debt. Meanwhile, if you are about to retire, and your investment portfolio is composed of conservative investments, the reverse could be better.

Making the decision if you want to invest or pay down debt will not only depend on your financial status but also on your economic situation. The key here is to set reachable financial goals, stay within your perspective, and assess your cash flow, risk tolerance, and investment choices.

Step 2: Learn the Basics of Investing

You don't have to be a financial expert to dabble in investing. However, you have to learn its basics so that you will be equipped and guided in making your decisions.

It is important to learn the differences between certificates of deposits (CDs), mutual funds, bonds, and stocks. You must also learn financial concepts like market efficiency, diversification, and portfolio optimization. You should also learn books that are written by ultra successful investors like Warren Buffett.

In this Chapter, we will discuss the basic elements of investing. With complicated theories and intimidating charts, the finance world could be really overwhelming. However, the stock market and the investment world will not be too difficulty to understand when you learn the basics and fundamental concepts.

However, you should remember that investing will not make you rich overnight. Organizing your personal finances requires effort, and of course there will always be a learning curve. But the rewards at stake will far outweigh the needed effort. You should not allow financial institutions, your boss, or investment experts take control of your money. You should learn as much as you can about finance because no one is in the best position than yourself in knowing what is best for you and your hard-earned money.

Regardless of your background, lifestyle, personality or interests, this Chapter will help you to understand the nature of investing, and how you can use it to earn money through the awesome concept of compounding. We will also discuss the building elements of the markets and the investing world, provide you some insight into strategies and techniques and help you think about which investment strategies will suit you best.

What Is Investing?

By its simple definition, investing is the practice of putting money to an instrument with the hope of getting profit in return. It is putting your money to work for you.

Investing is a different way to make money. Many of use believe that getting a job and working from 9 am to 5 pm is the only way to earn money. There's a major flaw in this structure, because if you want to make more money, you have to work for more hours. And more often than not, having a lot of money is not exciting as it sounds if you don't have the time to reap it.

Last time I checked, there is still no way to clone yourself so you can duplicate yourself and so double your working time. Hence, you can instead use money as an extension of yourself to work. In this structure, while you are working for your boss, or even enjoying tea in your garden, watching the latest film, or enjoying coffee with your friends, you are still earning money. Putting money to work for you could maximize your earning potential regardless if you receive a raise, work only four hours a day, or find another job with better pay.

There are numerous ways to put your money to work for you. This involves placing money into real estate, starting your own business, investing into mutual funds, buying bonds, or playing in the stock market.

People usually refer to these ways as investment vehicles, which is just a fancy way of referring to "ways to invest". Each way has its advantages and disadvantages, which you can learn more about in this book. It really doesn't matter which way you choose for investing your money. The objective is always to put your money to work so it could earn more profit for you. Although this is a very simple concept, it is the most fundamental concept that you should understand.

Investing Is Not Gambling

Remember, investing is not a form of gambling. Gambling is the practice of placing money at risk by placing on an uncertain result with the hope that you can win some money.

Some people cannot distinguish the difference between gambling and investing because they have used investment vehicles the wrong way. For instance, people buy stocks based on the "tips" they have heard from their friends while having lunch, which is the same as betting on a casino.

Real investing will never happen without exerting effort from your part. Real investors do not easily place money haphazardly on any investment. You should perform deep analysis and place money only if there is a high chance to get profits. Of course, there is still risk, and there are no 100% guarantee that you can earn the expected income. However, investing is more than simply wishing that Lady Luck smiles upon you.

Why Try Investing?

Most of us want to earn money. While it is not the most important thing in the world, earning a lot of money can make a difference. It is quite simple to understand that people are investing because they like to gain personal freedom, the capacity to buy thing they like, and be comfortable with the sense of security that money can provide.

But as time passes by, investing is now more of a necessity than luxury. The days when we can stay in a job for decades and then retire with a big pension are already gone. The government nowadays is always tightening its belt. Probably you have noticed that the obligation of retirement planning has gradually shifted from the state towards the citizens. Experts believe that our current pension system will not be enough after two decades. We should not leave it to chance. Through early planning, you can ensure your financial stability when you retire.

The Benefits of Compounding Interest

Now that you have at least a basic idea about investing, the next concept to understand is compound interest, which is considered as a mathematical miracle. In fact, Albert Einstein once said that compounding is the best mathematical discover of all time. I think you will later agree because not like calculus or trigonometry that most of us struggled in school, compounding has a practical application to our every day life.

The power of compounding can convert your working money into a tool that can generate income. Compounding refers to the process of earning money from money that has been reinvested. For compounding to work, it needs two things: time and the re-investment of profit. The longer the time you give your investments, the higher you can accelerate the potential income of your original capital that is actually taking the pressure off you.

Maybe the concept is still not that clear in your mind, so let's have an example:

Sam invested $10,000 at 6%. After one year, he will have $10,600 (because $10,000 x 1.06 = $10,600). Instead of withdrawing the profit, Sam decided to keep it for another year. If the interest rate is still at 6%, the investment will become $11,236.00 (because $10,600 x 1.06 = $11,236.00) at the end of year 2.

Because Sam decided to reinvest the $600, it will work together with the original investment, which will earn $636, which is $36 higher than the last year. This increase may seem very low after two years, but you should remember that you haven't exerted any effort to earn that money. In addition, this profit can earn more interest. At the end of the third year, Sam's investment will be $11,910 in total (because $11,236 × 1.06 = $11,910). Sam has already earned $674.16, and that is $74.16 more in interest than Year 1. This shows the power of compounding interest. This will continue as long as Sam decides to reinvest the money and keeps earning interest.

Step 3: Set Investment Goals

After sorting out your finances and understanding the basics of investing, the next step is to set your goals for investments. Although investment is all about making money, every investor came from different backgrounds and has different needs. You also need to consider the safety of capital, income, and appreciation of capital.

The best investment strategy for your will depend on your personal situation, lifestyle, and your age. A 33-year-old employee and a 65-year-old entrepreneur will have varying needs.

There are many investment choices available today, but each single investment vehicle could be categorized based on three fundamental types - growth, income, and safety. These categories also correspond to the kinds of investor goals. Although it is easy for an investor to have more than one of these goals, the success of one should come at the expense of other goals.

In this Chapter, we will evaluate the three objective types, the investments that you can use to achieve them as well as the ways that investors could integrate them in thinking of strategy.

David Weekly

Capital Growth or Capital Gains

Investment for growth can only be realized when the investment is sold for a price, which is higher than the original price. Capital loss, on the other hand, refers to the sales of a security at a lower price. Hence, investors who are searching for capital gains are often those who are in need of fixed, continuous investment source from their investment portfolio, but rather those who are searching the probability of long-lasting growth.

Capital growth is often associated with buying common stock, especially growth securities that offer minimal return but significant opportunity for increasing value. As such, regular stock is generally considered as a speculative investment as their return depends on what could happen in an uncertain future.

By contrast, blue-chip stocks can maximize your capital gains, which is generated by long-term increase in company revenues as well as profits as the company becomes more stable. But when it comes to safety and generating income, government bonds are the best investment vehicles.

You should also remember that capital gains provide possible tax advantages thanks to lower tax rate in many jurisdictions. For instance, funds that are generated through regular stock offerings are usually geared toward the growth plans of small companies, which is a process that is crucial for the growth of the country's economy. Therefore, to attract more people to invest in these areas, the government chooses to tax capital gains at a minimal rate compared to investments that are made because of income potential. This tax system serve to drive the culture of entrepreneurship and the growth of new businesses that are also helping in economic growth.

Income Investments

Investments with high percentage for safety often offer the cheapest rate of return. You should let go a degree of safety if you want to increase your revenue. This is actually the inverse relationship of yield and safety: as revenue increases, safety may go down, and the other way around.

To boost the rate of investment return as well as take on the risk associated with government bonds and money market instruments, you may chose to buy corporate bonds or preferred shares with lower ratings. Investment bonds with A or AA rating are a bit riskier compared to bonds with AAA grade, but they provide higher income yield compared to AAA grade. Likewise, bonds with BBB rating are though to carry medium risk but provide less potential yield compared to junk bonds that are offering the highest potential yield for bonds available but at the highest risk.

Many investors, even the conservative ones, still like to generate income from their investment portfolio. This is true even if it is just to keep up with the inflation rate of the economy. However, maximizing income yield could be an overarching concept for a portfolio, particularly for those who are in need of fixed total from their portfolio at least once a month. An investor who is already in retirement and needs a fixed amount of cash each month could be served by holding on to safe assets that can offer funds more than other assets that are generating income like pension and annuations.

Safe Investments

There is no such thing as a 100% safe and secure investment. But it is possible to choose investments that are safe by purchasing securities issued by the government in stable economic settings or by purchasing corporate bonds issued by the most stable companies. These investment securities offer the best way to maintain the principal capital while the investor can receive a specific rate for investing into them.

You can usually buy safe investments in the money market that includes securities like corporate bonds, government bonds, acceptance slips, commercial papers, certificate of deposits (CDs), and Treasury Bills or T-Bills. These securities have varying risk and potential returns. In order to compensate for the higher risk, the returns from the corporate bonds are higher than T-Bills.

It is crucial to understand that there's still a great range of risk in the bonds market. At one side of the spectrum, there are high-grade corporate and government bonds and on the other side there are junk bonds that carries high risk compared to some speculative stocks. To put it simply, it is not right to think that corporate bonds are absolutely safe. However, most investment vehicles from the money market can be regarded as highly safe.

Secondary Investment Goals

Liquidity or Marketability

Most of the investments mentioned above are not liquid to some degree as you cannot easily sold them and convert into cash. But attaining a level of liquidity may require you to sacrifice a specific degree of return or potential for capital growth.

Regular stock is usually regarded as the most liquid among investment vehicles, because you can easily sell it in hours. Bonds are also marketable, but there are bonds that are not liquid, because you cannot trade them within the fixed term. Likewise, you can only redeem money markets at the exact date at which the fixed term expires. If you are seeking liquidity, non-tradable bonds and money market assets are not ideal to be included in your portfolio.

Minimize Tax

You can pursue specific investments to minimize tax as part of your investment strategy. For instance, a business executive who earns six digits per month may like to seek investments within favorable tax consideration to minimize the total tax burden. Contributing to IRA or other investments that are sheltered from tax like 401(k) could be an effective strategy in minimizing tax.

As you may have realized by now, the benefits of one investment vehicle usually comes at the expense of advantages of another. If you are seeking for growth, for example, you may need to sacrifice and income. Hence, most portfolios could be guided by one encompassing objective that all other potential goals carrying less significant value in the whole investment spectrum.

Selecting an investment objective for your strategy and allocating value to all other goals is a process, which will depend on other factors like your temperament, civil status, financial background, age, and more. Among the many possibilities, you can surely find the right diversity of investment vehicles for your portfolio. But it is crucial to find, study, and decide on the opportunities that could match your goals.

What Is Your Purpose in Investing?

Like any business activity, investing should be done with direction. Clarifying your purposes or reasons for investing is crucial to ensure that this activity will be fruitful. Similar to working out in a gym, investing could become tedious, difficult, and even risky if you don't work toward a goal and you are not keeping track of your progress. Below are the most common purposes for investment:

Retirement

Again, you should not depend your retirement years to the government. No one knows if the current pension system could support our needs when we are weak and sick!

You should plan your own retirement. Try reading the news today and you will see updates about companies freezing pensions or new legislation to cut government bailouts. In these times of uncertainty, investing can be a great tool to help you plan your retirement. There are three rules that you should know:

1. The earlier you you begin learning about investments, the easier it will be to pick up. It can be difficult and expensive to choose and keep financial advisors. Hence, it is best to handle your own investment affairs.

2. The older you start, the higher your risk aversion. If you are already in your golden years, you may need to use guaranteed investments like debt securities that are only offering minimum returns. In contrast, if you begin young, you could still survive a setback even if your investments fail.

3. The more years between your current age and your retirement age, the longer you have to grow your money. Bear in mind that you need to fight inflation if you are planning for retirement. To put it simply, if you don't invest your instruments to combat inflation, it will not be worth as much after several decades.

Investment for your retirement is quite similar to long-term investing. You have to find high-quality investment vehicles to purchase and keep with the majority of your capital. You should aim to diversify your retirement portfolio to include index funds, debt securities, stocks, and other instruments from the money market. This diversity will change as you do eventually moving to low-risk investments as you become older.

Attaining Financial Objectives

Investing is not always for the long-term. You can use it as a tool to improve your current financial status as well as shaping your financial future. Probably you like to buy a new car next year or go on an luxury Asian cruise? Your holiday will feel more rewarding if you pay it using your dividends.

You can use investing to improve your income, which will help you to buy the things that you like. Because investing may change along with your goals, this kind of investment is not for retirement investment. Investing to attain financial goals includes a mix of short-term and long-term investments. If you are putting your money to work in the hope of buying a bigger house after five years, then you can achieve this if you invest in long-term instruments. If you like to invest so you can buy a new gadget at the end of the year, you may consider short-term instruments that are offering high returns.

The key here is you need to identify your financial goals first. If you like to go on a luxury cruise this summer, you need to sit down and determine the cost of this holiday and then find your investment strategy to meet this goal. Without setting your goal first, the money which should be invested into that purpose might be used for other allocations like holiday splurges.

It can be challenging and exciting to invest in order to achieve your financial goals. Mixing the strain of time limits with the idea that you are not familiar in managing large capitals of money like investing for retirement, you could be less averse to risk and so you are more motivated to learn more about high yield investments like shorting and growth stocks. And the good thing is, you can expect a nice reward at the end.

Why Not Invest?

There are also two major reasons why you should not invest: insufficient knowledge and debt.

First, you should not jump into the world of investment if you don't have enough knowledge of the instruments and the financial systems that make this world go round. Pouring your money into investments that you are not familiar is like burning your money. Why would you enter into a gym and lift 150 lbs during your first day (unless you have already developed the needed muscles). Your first try in investing must follow similar incremental journey as working out in the gym.

Second, you should not jump into investments if you are neck-deep in debt. Let's say you have $3000 loan at 13% interest, and you received $3000 as a year-end bonus. Should you use the money to buy stocks or pay the loan? You should go with the latter. Pay the loan! If you choose to buy stocks, your capital should yield a return of more than 9% exclusive of the fees and commissions to make the investment a better option. This is possible, but it is a bit easier to look for good returns on investments without struggling with the possible losses on the loan.

There are various types of debt - loan sharks, student loans, mortgage, credit card - and they carry varying levels of weight if you are to decide whether to invest despite having debt.

Your investment purposes may change as you go through your life. This is a crucial process, because the only other choice is to jump into investment without purpose that may possibly lead in investing processes that mirror your uncertainty and affect the returns. You need to review and adjust your goals and reasons as your life changes.

Even if the changes in your life are nothing significant, it is always ideal to review your goals regularly to see your progress. Like going to the gym, investing will be easier when you actually get up and start.

Step 4: Determine Your Risk Tolerance

Before deciding on which type of investments are suitable for you, it is crucial first to know how much risk you are willing to assume. Are you excited of riding a fast bike and enjoy the risk, or do you like reading a nice book while enjoying the warm afternoon in your backyard? Risk tolerance may vary depending on your financial goals, income requirements, and age.

The topic of risk tolerance basically revolve around two questions:

- How much risk could you handle?
- How much risk must you take on?

The usual answer to Question 1 is not often similar to the answer to Question 2, although some financial experts may think it is. The first question is more about risk tolerance - how comfortable you are about the movement of your investment portfolios. But just because you can take a risk, doesn't necessarily mean that you should. Here comes the second question. Unluckily, risk tolerance is usually considered as the key factor in determining the portfolio's asset allocation.

In this chapter, you will learn more about the factors that you should consider in setting up an investment strategy for the long term: the optimal risk, risk for capacity, and risk tolerance.

Optimal Risk

Optimal risk is applicable to the creation of portfolios that are risk-efficient. The portfolio's optimal risk rises from the modern portfolio theory. Central to this theory is the idea that investors are working to lessen the risk or variance while they are also working to increase yield.

In the modern portfolio theory, there is an ideal mix of asset classes. This refers to the point where adding another risk will provide the highest marginal return. If you put this another way, it is the point you can get the most return for your risk.

Risk for Capacity

In applying the idea of risk when it comes to investment, there are actually two kinds of risk-relevant attributes that are distinctive. The first is a psychological characteristic known as risk tolerance that you will learn later. The other refers to the capacity of the investor to tolerate risk.

You can measure financial risk capacity in numerous ways, including the income, wealth, liquidity, and time horizon. Investors who are looking for high liquidity are limited to how much risk they could take. They are pushed to stay away from investments, which could be possibly lucrative because they don't provide the needed liquidity. In the long run, the market volatility could be dampened, and the returns could move toward long-term historical averages. The longer the horizon for time, the higher the risk capacity of the investors as the market's short-term volatility may lose its significance.

Risk Tolerance

Risk Tolerance refers your willingness to be receptive to volatility or higher risk in return for higher possible yield. Those who have high tolerance are considered aggressive investors, because they are willing to lose their capital in seeking for higher yield. Those who have low tolerance or risk-averse, are considered as conservative investors who are more interested in preserving capital. The difference is only justified by your level of comfort.

If your risk tolerance is high, you can pursue higher possible reward investments even if there's a higher possibility of losing capital. A risk-tolerant investor may choose not to forego of stocks in a temporary market adjustment, while a risk-averse investor could search out for high-risk investments even if they only yield minimal returns.

Risk tolerance measures the level of risk that you could handle. However, this is not necessarily the same as the suitable amount of risk that you should take.

If your cash flow is in perfect health, you can search for higher-risk investments because they have funds coming in regardless of the conditions of the market. Likewise, beginners with limited capital to invest may still have the capacity for high risk, since they still have enough time for recovery even if they lost.

You could wait out any short-term fall, which lowers the opportunity of the need to withdraw before the market could bounce back.

How Much Risk Must You Take On?

For many investors, optimal risk, risk for capacity, and risk tolerance are aligned closely to each other. To put this simply, they are close to each other on the efficient spectrum. But for some investors, the balance doesn't necessarily mean alignment.

Usually when investors meet with investment advisor, they are asked to answer some questions about risk tolerance. However, there are three major flaws in this practice:

1. Risk tolerance may not align with real financial status. What you could tolerate psychologically may be greater compared to your financial capacity. For instance, if you want to trade futures, you may psychologically manage the volatility, but a sizeable bet, which goes wrong could easily wipe you out.

2. The questions could be all hypothetical. In real life setting, you may behave differently than you assume you will behave when faced with adversity. Answering a questionnaire about what you will feel if your stocks plummets is much different compared to actually experiencing it.

3. A portfolio based on risk tolerance may not meet your financial goals. For instance, an investor who is risk-averse could end up with a portfolio that may not be worth enough to support him during retirement.

It is crucial that the financial capacity must be the dominant factor. You must never take more risk than what you can absorb. For example, if you need the money next week, you should not invest all your capital to the stock market today. If your present financial situation doesn't allow you to handle a sudden downfall, then you should avoid the risk. You should strive for the optimal risk point if there is a good tradeoff between reward and risk.

Step 5: Find Your Investment Style

After knowing your risk tolerance and investment goals, the next step is to find your style in investing. Most starting investors may find that their risk tolerance and their goals will usually not match up. For instance, if you prefer fast cars but you are searching for safety of your money, you may take a more conservative approach to investing.

Those who are conservative will usually invest at least 70% of their money in low-risk, fixed income securities like T-bills, with 15% allocated to blue chip equities. Aggressive investors, on the other hand, may invest as much as 100% of their capital on equities.

How to Achieve Optimal Asset Allocation

Allocating your capital among various classes of assets is a critical strategy to assist in minimizing risk and possibly increase gains. You can regard this as the contra-concept of putting all eggs in a single basket. The first step in understanding optimal asset allocation is to define its purpose, then take a closer look at how allocation can be advantageous for your investment, and the right asset mix to achieve and keep it.

Asset Allocation - Definition and Purpose

Asset allocation refers to the strategy of classifying your portfolio across different classes of assets such as money market securities, bonds, and stocks. Basically, asset allocation is an effective method to diversify your investments.

Your options will usually fall within three classes - cash, bonds, and stocks. Under these three classes are sub-classes in which there are further variations within every category. Common alternatives and subclasses are the following:

- **Small Cap Stocks** - These are stocks representing small businesses with a market cap of not more than $2 Billion. These equities have the tendency to have the highest volatility because of lower liquidity.

- **Mid Cap Stock** - Medium enterprises offer these stocks with a market cap not larger than $10 Billion but not less than $2 Billion

- **Large Cap Stock** - These are stocks offered by large companies with a market capital usually higher than $10 Billion.

- **Emerging Markets** - This class indicates securities from the financial markets of a developing nation. Even though investments in developing countries provide higher potential yield, the volatility is also higher, usually because of lower liquidity and political instability.

- **Money Market Securities** - These are debt securities that are highly liquid, which you can redeem after a year. This category is mainly composed of T-Bills and government bonds.

- **International Securities** - These assets are offered by international corporations and included on forex. International securities will allow you to diversify investments beyond your country of origin. However, these securities also carry high country risk. This risk mainly runs from the possibility that a state may not have the capacity to recognize its financial agreements.

- **Real Estate Investment Trusts (REITs)** - You can trade REITs like you trade equities. The difference is on the underlying asset as a share of properties and mortgages instead of shares from a company.

- **Fixed Income Securities** - This class is composed of debt securities, which will pay you a fixed amount of return, at maturity or on schedule, and also the capital return once the security reaches maturity. This class usually has lower risk compared to equities, and has less risk due to the stable return that they can provide. Take note that even though payment of income is guaranteed by the issuing entity, there is always the default risk. This class of investment includes government bonds and corporate bonds.

Minimizing Risk and Maximizing Returns

Remember, the primary goal of asset allocation is to reduce risk given a specific expected level of return. Of course, to minimize risk and maximize return, you have to understand the risk-return trait of the different classes of assets.

The idea behind this is the risk-return tradeoff that refers to the possible increase in return carrying also an increase in risk. Hence, diversification by allocating asset is crucial. Because different assets also have different risks as well as market fluctuation, suitable allocation of asset could insulate the whole portfolio from the rise and fall of one class of security.

Hence, while a portion of the portfolio could contain securities that are highly volatile that you might have chosen because of their potential returns - the other side of your portfolio allocated to other assets are still stable. Because of the protection that it provides, asset allocation is important in minimizing risk while maximizing returns.

Choosing What Is Right for You

As every asset class has different levels of risk and return, you should look at your available capital, time horizon, investment goals and risk tolerance as basis for your asset allocation.

If you have larger capital to invest or if you have longer time horizon, you might be more comfortable with high return, high-risk investments. On the other hand, if you have low cash capital and shorter time horizon, you might be more comfortable with low return, low risk allocations.

Most investment companies create a series of portfolios, each composing various proportions of asset classes. This is to make the allocation of asset a bit easier for investors. These portfolios of various proportions satisfy a certain level of risk tolerance for investors. Generally, these portfolios may range from highly aggressive to conservative.

Highly Aggressive Portfolios

Highly aggressive portfolios are composed mostly of equities. Hence, with a highly aggressive portfolio, the primary goal is high growth of capital over longer period. Because these portfolios carry a considerable level of risk, the portfolio value may vary widely in shorter period of time.

Aggressive Portfolios

Aggressive portfolios are primarily composed of equities, so their value has the tendency to fluctuate often. If you want to consider aggressive portfolios, your primary objective should be to gain long-term capital growth. Hence, the strategy of an aggressive portfolio is usually known as capital growth strategy. If you want to diversity, you can add several securities that are on fixed-income.

Mildly Aggressive Portfolios

Mildly aggressive portfolios are usually known as balanced portfolios, because the composition of the asset is divided equally between equities and fixed income securities to allow balance of income and growth. Because mildly aggressive portfolios carry high level of risk compared to conservative portfolios, this strategy is ideal for investors with longer time allowance (often longer than five years), and a mild level of risk tolerance.

Mildly Conservative Portfolios

A mildly conservative portfolio is suitable if you want to maintain a large percentage of the portfolio's value but still you are open to take a higher level of risk to protect from inflation. A usual strategy within this risk is known as "current income strategy", which allows you to invest on securities that can yield high returns.

Conservative Portfolios

In general, conservative portfolios allocate a high percentage of the total portfolio to lower risk securities like money market and fixed-income securities. The primary objective in investing in a conservative portfolio is to safeguard its main value (your original cash capital). Hence, investing in this portfolio is known as capital preservation strategy.

Even if you want to be a conservative investor and you want to stay away from investing in stock market, some exposure could help you avoid inflation. You can choose to invest in equity portion in high-yield blue chip companies or index fund, because the objective is not to beat the market.

Customize Your Asset Allocations According to Your Needs

Remember, the portfolios described above as well as the strategies for investment are only loose guides. You can always change your portfolios according to your individual needs and strategies. The way you adjust the models above will depend on your future needs for cash and what type of investor you are. For example, if you prefer to research your own companies and devote your time for picking stocks, then you can further allocate equities portion of your portfolio among stocks subclasses.

In addition, the money market vehicles and the amount of cash you have in your portfolio will be based on the level of liquidity and safety you want. If you like investments, which you can easily liquidate, or you like to keep the present value of your portfolio, then you may want to put a bigger allocation of your investment portfolio in the short-term fixed income or money market securities.

Step 6: Know the Associated Costs in Investment

It is crucial to know the costs associated in investing, because specific costs may cut into the returns of your investment. In general, strategies for passive investing tend to have lower fees compared to strategies for active investing like stock trading. Take note that stockbrokers will charge commissions. If you are beginning with a smaller cash capital, a discount broker can be a good choice, because they will only charge a minimal commission.

Meanwhile, if you are buying mutual funds, take note that funds charge several administrative fees including the cost of managing the fund, and some funds may also charge load fees.

As you might have already surfed online for basic information on mutual funds, you might have already encountered some posts about the advantages of choosing no-load mutual funds. In this Chapter, we will explore the differences between the load and no-load funds.

Load Mutual Funds

Load mutual funds refers to the funds that you can buy from your broker or advisors with commission or sales charge. This includes the payment for the middleman for his time and expertise in choosing the right funds, which usually have back-end, front end or sales charge, depending on the specific class of shared purchase. Moreover, a load mutual fund may also carry 12b-1 fee, which could be as high as 1% of the net asset value or NAV of the fund.

No Load Mutual Funds

You can get no-load at NAV without the need to pay level sales charges. You can buy shares either indirectly from a mutual fund market or directly from a company selling mutual funds. These funds may carry a minimal 12b-1 fee, also regarded as distribution cost that is already integrated into the expense ratio of the fund. You can pay the expense ratio regularly through a reduction in the price of the fund. There are also available no-load funds that don't carry 12b-1 fees when bought directly from a company. These funds are usually referred to as true no-load mutual funds.

The Advantages of Choosing No-Load Mutual Funds

According to studies, no-load funds have the strength to beat load funds over a given time. For instance, based on a study conducted by Craig Israelsen and published in the Financial Planning Journal, you may need to pay for the extra services that you will receive for investing in load mutual funds. Israelsen used data from the Morningstar, which covered the financial turbulence between 2000 and 2002 when the S&P 500 plummeted to almost 35%.

The study revealed that no load funds greatly outperformed load funds within the time period. The superiority of the no-load mutual fund was between 10 and 430 base points with noticeable performance in the small capital classes. Moreover, the study also revealed that no load funds beaten the load funds in every category of the Morningstar style during the financial crisis. The underlying logic is quite simple for this: if you are buying a fund for a lower price without the fees compared to a load fund, your profits will be higher.

Still, Load Funds Can Also Be Great Investments

It seems that it is better to buy no-load mutual funds, right? After all, who will pay a sales fee if you not needed? But there are still great reasons why you should still invest in load mutual funds.

Most investors, especially those who are just starting in the fields are not confident in choosing investments, and so they need the help of financial advisors. Financial advisors usually encourage people to invest on mutual funds that have been performing well. Investment decisions should be backed up by research, and most people don't have the luxury of time to delve into deep analysis. Also, carving out time to manage investments could be a bit challenging especially for busy individuals.

There are also investors who are maintaining connections with their advisors and they don't like to taint this connection by looking for direct investments. They also like the one-stop investing option that a broker may provide. Meanwhile, there are investors who like to play the blame game so they are looking for investors to blame when their investment goes awry.

Some investors also need the guidance of financial advisors and brokers especially during turbulent times in the market.

In spite of the charges, and to some extent, lower yields, load funds can still be great addition to your portfolio, especially if you are just a beginner or you got no time in managing your funds. In the end, you have to decide if the services you could avail are valuable enough to give up the higher returns of a no-load fund.

Step 7: Find Your Investment Advisor

Whether you don't have the luxury of time to analyze investment vehicles or you feel that you need an expert opinion, getting the help of an investment advisor could help you a lot.

However, you should not rush and hire the first investment advisor you meet. Selecting a financial advisor is like buying a car. It is one of the biggest financial decisions you need to make. Hence, you should consider numerous factors, and get to know your requirements before you buy. In this Chapter, we will take a closer look on the important pointers you should consider if you are in the market of finding an investment advisor.

First Impression

A good first impression is crucial in buying a car, and you can often make a good impression by the design of the car. Similarly, investment advisors make their impression by their designations. Their professional experience is shaped by the level of education they have attained. The higher their level of education, the more there is to signify that the advisor has comprehensive knowledge and dedication to the industry.

But like some cars that have great designs but also have the tendency to fall down to rust, an investment advisor may have their designations great but are really limited in capacity. Many certifications are now available, and not all have the same weight. Hence, you need to ensure that you know the significance of these designations.

Performance

You might probably consider brand reputation in deciding to purchase a car. Some may still choose the proven brands that have been in the industry for years, while others may try a new brand. Likewise, you might want to look for a financial advisor who has a proven track record, or you might decide to try a new advisor who is just building his reputation. More often than not, investment advisors who have been in the industry for decades are more expensive to hire compared to newbies with only a few years of experience in their belt. This doesn't mean that newly graduates will not help you to make money, but they carry more risk.

Experience can be an asset for advisors, but a long experience will not worth much if it is not a great one. Be sure that you find out if your prospective advisor had numerous complaints, and discover what actions he took to resolve them. It is okay to look into the track record of the advisor, but you can also ask him personally.

Relationship

A great customer service policy should include a willingness to take care of your concerns. This is crucial in any kind of customer-investor relationship. Your investment advisor should show willingness to be open with you. Be sure to ask the following questions when you are assessing your relationship with an investment advisor:

- Doe she have a plan to meet with you or at least communicate regularly?

- Is there a regular schedule to review your investments or will the advisor call you only if there are bad concerns?

- Does the advisor show strong willingness to understand your goals, and is willing to guide you on how you can achieve these goals?

The variability of the product could be a bit complicated. Just like a car agent working for Ford will not encourage you to buy Audi, an advisor will not likely push you to look at the offers fro other companies. But this doesn't mean that your advisor must not look out for your interests. In order to do this, he must have a certain level of independence. Be sure to figure out if the advisor is occupied with helping you yield returns or committed to make large returns for an investment company.

Investment Options

When you choose a car, going on several options will directly depend on your needs. You should not pay for an expensive model if you don't need its features. If you live in Florida, does the block heater beneficial to you, or if you are in Alaska, do you really need high-end air conditioning?

Choosing an investment advisor will be easier if you are clear on your goals and needs. While the core of investment is usually similar anywhere in the market, the options that are available for you could make a difference. You can make a list of what you need from your potential advisor, and then figure out if he provides you the suitable services for the price you can pay.

Deciding on the right investment advisor, like choosing the right car is a crucial step requiring you to do your due diligence and shop around. However, you also need to consider what you can expect and what you need.

Take note that this book is only providing you a basic guideline of what you have to consider. So be sure to set aside enough time and ensure that you can cover the grounds. You will regret choosing a too expensive car that can't service your needs. Similarly, a bad decision on an investment advisor could be a long-term liability. A poor investment advisor may not only become a useless expense, but may also cause for lost returns, lost chances to make money, or even lost chance to sleep well at night.

Step 8: Choose Your Investments

After the preludes, here comes the exciting step: choosing your investments. If you want to be conservative with your investments, you should fill your portfolio with income-producing, low-risk securities like money market funds and federal bonds. You should take note of diversification and asset allocation. When you diversify your investment into various classes of assets, you can stay away from the problems related to putting all your eggs into a single basket. By allocating your assets, on the other hand, you can balance the risk as well as the reward by allocating your capital between the three classes of assets: cash, fixed-income, and equities.

Steps in Building a Profitable Portfolio

In the current financial marketplace, it is crucial to maintain your investment portfolio so you can become successful. When you start investing, you should know how you can identify an allocation, which can best conform to your personal investment goals as well as strategies. To put it simply, your investment portfolio must also meet your future needs for cash and prevent you from being anxious that your investments may fail. You can create portfolios aligned to your investment goals and strategies by following a strategic approach. Below are the steps in building a portfolio that will provide you high profit:

Step 1: Figure Out the Ideal Asset Allocation According to Your Needs

Evaluating your financial status and your investment objectives is the first step in creating a profitable portfolio. Vital factors to consider are your future capital needs, capital to invest, time horizon, and your age. A young professional who is just starting his career and a 45-year-old married man who need to send his two kids to college and has plans for early retirement will have very distinctive strategies for their investments.

You should also consider your risk tolerance and personality. Are you open to take on the risk of investing your capital for the probability of getting high returns? All investors, of course, like to reap high yields for their investments. However, if you are the type of person who can't sleep at night because of a sudden drop in your investments, then the high profit from these types of assets may not be worth the anxiety.

Getting a clear view of your present situation as well as your future capital needs, and your risk tolerance will help you figure out how you allocate your investments among various classes of assets. The probability of higher returns comes at the expense of higher risk of losses, which is a principle regarded as the risk/return tradeoff. You should not stay away from the risk so you can maximize it according to your unique style and condition.

For instance, if you are young and your need for future capital is low, you can afford to take higher risks in your expectation for higher profits. Meanwhile, if you are near your retirement age you need to concentrate on guarding your assets and attracting income from these assets while minimizing taxes.

Step 2: Follow the Investment Strategy According to Your Plan in Step 1

After determining the ideal asset allocation, you just need to categorize your capital between the right asset classes. This can be easy: bonds are bonds and equities are equities.

However, it is still possible to divide the various classes of assets into sub-categories that also have various risks as well as possible returns. For instance, you may slash the portion of the equity between various market caps and sectors, and between foreign and domestic stocks. The portion of the bond may be appointed between long term and short term, corporate debt versus government debt, etc.

There are different ways that you could go about selecting the securities and assets in order to achieve your strategy for asset allocation. Be sure to evaluate the potential and quality of every investment you purchase, because not all stocks and bonds carry the same features and risks.

Bonds

You need to consider several factors in choosing bonds: interest rate, type of bond, rating, maturity, and coupon.

Stocks

Select stocks according to the risk level that you like to shoulder the equity portion of investment portfolio. The factors to consider are type of stock, market cap as well as sector. Evaluate the businesses through stock filters to get a shortlist of possible picks, and then do a comprehensive analysis on every possible purchase to assess its risks and opportunities to go forward. This is considered as the most work-comprehensive way of including securities on portfolio. You may need to monitor the price fluctuations from time to time and stay updated about the company and the industry.

Mutual Funds

You can invest in mutual funds that are available in different classes of assets, and will let you buy bonds and stocks that have been studied and chosen by experts or fund managers. But remember, these fund managers will ask payment for their professional services that will be deducted from your stock earnings. Another option is investing into index funds, which have lower service charge, as they reflect a stable index and so they are managed passively.

Exchange Traded Funds (ETFs)

When you choose to stay away from mutual funds, Exchange Traded Funds could be a better alternative. ETFs are like mutual funds, because they signify a sizeable bundle of stocks -

typically categorized by country, capitalization, and sector. The difference is that these are managed passively, but rather follow a selected index. Because of this passive management, ETFs are more affordable compared to mutual funds but still you can take advantage of the benefits of diversification.

Step 3: Re-evaluate the Weightings of Your Portfolio

When you have established your investment portfolio, you have to evaluate and rebalance it regularly because the movements in the market could cause the initial value to fluctuate. To evaluate the actual asset allocation of the portfolio, you can categorize the investments and assess the proportions of the whole value.

The factors that may change over time include your risk tolerance, future needs, and your present financial status. If these things change, you may have to adjust your portfolio. When your risk tolerance becomes low, you may have to decrease the amount of equities you are holding. Or maybe, you are now more receptive of higher risks and your allocation on assets may require that a small percentage of your assets be held in small-cap stocks.

In order to rebalance, you have to figure out which of your positions are undervalued, and which of the are overvalued. For instance, let's say that you have 35% of your existing assets in small-cap equities, and your asset allocation shows that you must only have 20% of your assets in this class. Through rebalancing, you can figure out how much of this position you have to decrease and allocate to other types of classes.

Step 4: Rebalance Your Portfolio

After determining which securities you have to reduce and by how much, you also have to decide which undervalued securities you will purchase with the returns from selling the overvalued securities. In order to select your securities, you can use the approaches described in Step 2.

In selling assets for portfolio rebalancing, be sure to consider the effects on your taxes when you readjust your portfolio. Possibly, the investment in growth stocks could strongly increase in the past year. However, if you will sell all your equities to rebalance your portfolio, you may have to incur considerable taxes on capital gains. In this situation, you may just avoid contributing to any additional funds to this asset class while continue your contributions to other asset classes. This will decrease the value of your growth stocks over a certain period without incurring too many taxes for your capital gains.

Meanwhile, you should also consider the status of your securities. If you think that those same overvalued growth stocks may just fall, you have to sell despite of the possible implications on your taxes. Expert opinions and securities reports can guide you to help you evaluate the outlook for your holdings. Tax-loss selling is also a strategy that you could use to minimize the implications on your taxes.

You can learn more about rebalancing your investment portfolio in the next chapter.

Remember to Diversify

For the whole process of constructing your portfolio, it is important that you remember to diversify your allocation of assets. Don't just buy securities from every asset class. You should also diversify within every class. Make certain that you distribute your holdings in a specific asset class across a range of industry sectors and subclasses.

Take note that you can achieve great diversification by investing into ETFs and mutual funds. These investment channels will allow you to obtain the economies of scale that professional fund managers could take advantage.

In general, a diversified investment portfolio is your greatest asset for continuous, long-term investment growth. It will safeguard your assets from the risks of high declines as well as changes in the economy. Regularly keep track of the diversification of your investment portfolio, make adjustments if needed, and you will significantly increase your chances for long-term success in investing.

Step 9: Review Your Investments

The final phase in your investing journey is re-assessing your investment portfolio. When you have already finalized your strategy for allocating your assets, you may realize that the value of your assets may have changes over a certain period of time. This usually happens if the value of different securities within your investment portfolio has changed. You can easily modify this by rebalancing your investments.

The Process of Rebalancing Your Investments

Rebalancing refers to the process of trading portions of your investments to set the value of every asset class back to its initial state. Moreover, if your tolerance risk of investment strategy has significantly changed, you can rebalance your portfolio to readjust the value of every asset class or security to achieve a newly devised allocation for your asset.

The investment mix that you initially created will inevitably change because of the various returns among different asset classes and securities. Hence, the portion that you have allocated to various asset classes will also change, which may affect the risk level of your investment portfolio. Hence, it is crucial to compare a readjusted portfolio to one where the changes were overlooked. You should also look at the possible effects of ignored allocations in an investment portfolio.

The Effects of Imbalance

A common belief among numerous investors is that if a portfolio has performed well in the previous year, it will also perform well the next year. But alas, previous performance is not a great indication of good performance in the future. Still, many investors invest heavily in the winning funds of the previous years and choose to reduce the value of their investments in the losing funds of the previous years. Take note that equities have high volatility compared to securities on fixed-income. Hence, the large gains of the previous years could translate into losses for the next year.

Rebalancing Your Portfolio

The frequency of rebalancing your investment portfolio will depend on your tax implications, personal preferences, as well as service fees. It also includes the type of account that you are trading and if your capital losses or gains will be taxed. Rebalancing your portfolio at least once a year is enough. But some assets in your portfolio may not experience a significant appreciation in a year, so longer time horizon may be suitable. In addition, changes in your lifestyle may also mean change to your strategies for allocating assets. Regardless of your preference, be sure to remember of the following guidelines in rebalancing your investment portfolio:

Record the Changes

If you have just decided to follow a strategy for trading securities in every asset class, you should keep a record of the total value of every security at that particular time including the total value of your portfolio. This will serve as your reference for historical data, so it will be easy for you to compare the past and current values.

Compare the Previous and Present Values

On a specific fate in the future, you can compare the present value of your portfolio and of every class of asset. Compute the value of every fund in your portfolio by dividing the present value of every asset class by the total present value of the portfolio. Compare the result to the original value. Have you noticed considerable change? If not, and if there is no requirement to liquidate your investment for your short-term needs, you can choose not to implement any adjustments.

Adjust Your Portfolio

If you discover that there are significant changes in the value of your class assets, and this change exposed your portfolio to risk, then take the present total value of your portfolio and multiply this by every percentage value initially assigned to every class of the assets. The result refers to the amount that you should invest in every asset class to keep the initial asset allocation. Maybe you have to trade securities from classes whose values are very high and buy more securities in classes whose values decreased.

Rebalancing your investment portfolio could help you keep the original allocation for your asset and let you make any changes according to your investment goals and strategies. Basically, rebalancing your portfolio could help you follow your investment plans regardless of the situation in the market.

Conclusion

The world of investing can be a dangerous place for starters. It is a jungle out there with many wild animals and toxic plants that could put your life in danger. But still, many are exploring this wilderness in search of great rewards - wealth, freedom, or just the thrill out of it.

Regardless of your intentions why you want to invest, you should always equip yourself with the right knowledge and skills so you can be successful in this industry. That is why you should always strive for continuous learning. Read more books, learn investing strategies and tactics, join investing networks both online and offline, and continue practicing what you have learned.

Finally, if you enjoyed this book, please take the time to share your thoughts and post a positive review on Amazon. It'd be greatly appreciated!

Thank you and good luck!

www.ingramcontent.com/pod-product-compliance
Lightning Source LLC
Chambersburg PA
CBHW060412190526
45169CB00002B/867